A BRIEF HISTORY

OF

THE HUGUENOTS

The Rev. Herbert L. Stein-Steinschneider, Ph.D.

Pastor of the French Protestant Church of Washington, DC

Pastor of the Huguenot Church, Charleston, SC

President, the Lafayette-Rochambeau Society

Washington, DC

1981

A Brief History of the Huguenots
Copyright © 2018 Cool F/X Publishing
ISBN: 978-0-9863963-0-4

All rights reserved. Parts of the publication may be reproduced, stored in a retrieval system, or transmitted in any form by means electrical, mechanical, or otherwise, but it would be nice if one would also let the editor know that this was being done.

TABLE OF CONTENTS

FOREWARD ii
INTRODUCTION vi
THE FIRST REFORMATION 1
JOHN CALVIN (1509-1564) 4
THE HUGUENOT TRADITION 8
THE NAME "HUGUENOT" 12
THE HUGUENOT CROSS 14
THE MEREAU 17
THE FLAGS OF THE HUGUENOTS 18
HUGUENOT HISTORY 21
   1. The Feudal Period (1536-1572) 21
   2. The Democratic Period (1572-1628) 29
   3. Religious Period (1628-1685) 34
THE WALLOONS 38
   1. The Huguenot "Underground" (1685-1787) 41
THE HUGUENOT DISPERSION 50

FOREWARD

In the 1970s, while I was a small boy, my father self-published *A Brief History of the Huguenots*, which he distributed to friends and other interested parties. It was produced on an old A.B. Dick mimeograph machine, with which various editions were published in 1975, 1977, and 1981.

The title page of this book reflects the last year dad issued this book. He was also still pastor at the French Church of Washington, DC; pastor of the Huguenot Church in Charleston, South Carolina; President of the Lafayette-Rochambeau Society; and also, Professor of Religion at the German School in Potomac, Maryland at the time. In fact, when he died from a heart attack on March 9, 1990, he had been pastor there for 40 years as well as the founder of numerous groups and associations. He was the epitome of a Renaissance Man.

My father started spelling his last name "Stein-Schneider" as soon as he arrived in America in 1947 to attend the Theological Seminary at Princeton. Ostensibly, it was to make the long name easier for Americans to pronounce. Later in life I discovered that the name was originally written as "Steinschneider," so I have reverted to this.

Over the years, people have asked for copies of this short book. An original copy even appeared on Amazon.com for an exorbitant price at one time. After my father's death, however, access to the material was essentially lost, as we had no idea where the originals could be found, so making the book available was impossible.

After going through boxes of papers I had consolidated and stored decades since my dad's passing, I stumbled on copies of this book. A few original hard copies were sent to those who had requested them.

Eventually, I scanned one of the originals, ran the outputs through optical character recognition software, and began editing the results with the intention of making this available again.

Unfortunately, other projects got in the way. But the time has finally come to offer this to all that have asked. And hopefully, those who are interested in the history of the

Huguenots will also find the account useful.

It would have pleased my father to know that his little labor of love finally made it to the formal printing press and is now available to everyone in the world.

Phil Steinschneider

INTRODUCTION

This brief account of Huguenot history is dedicated to all those who find inspiration in the dramatic events of the past and in the steadfast faith of their forbearers. May these pages prompt you to pride in your Huguenot ancestors – and make your own faith in Jesus Christ as unshakeable as was theirs.

Strong interest in Huguenot ancestry and history started in the United States only toward the end of the 19th century, when wealth and leisure prompted Americans to explore their national and religious roots. Historians of great caliber, such as Baird and Parkman, wrote about the Huguenots and their past. They produced authoritative books on the subject.

Soon those who shared interest in these French Reformed roots united in societies. New York (1883), South Carolina (1885), and Pennsylvania (1918) were the leaders. Not too long thereafter, a number of state Societies united into the National Huguenot Society. This organization holds its annual National Congress in Washington D.C. and celebrates on this occasion a Huguenot religious service in the original French, singing the great Huguenot Psalms in the original language.

A "World Huguenot Center" was created in Paris shortly after World War II, when Huguenot descendants from England, Germany, the United States, and many other nations expressed an interest in a central organization of the worldwide movement. An international Congress and Huguenot Pilgrimage is organized by the World Huguenot Center every three years. Paris, Strasbourg, La Rochelle, and Rouen have been the sites in the past. Many American Huguenots have attended these most inspirational meetings.

The World Huguenot Center is located at 47 Rue de Clichy, 75008 Paris, France. Its actual Secretary General is Thierry du Pasquier, a noted genealogist, who visited the American Huguenot Societies in 1976.

The uniquely important center of research into Huguenot history is the Library of the "Société d'Histoire du Protestantisme Français," located at 54 Rue des Saints-Pères 75007 Paris, France. In the United States, the

Library of Congress preserves invaluable material. The National Huguenot Society published in 1975 a roster of Huguenot ancestors compiled by Mrs. G. Cobb and edited by Nicholas Ward of Washington D.C.

A note about Huguenot music: A number of Huguenot Psalms (melody only) are contained in the Episcopal Hymnal of 1940. They can be identified by the composer's name, Loys Bourgeois. The Presbyterian Hymnal contains a single, lonely Huguenot tune, the Old Hundredth. The French Reformed Church of France edits a Huguenot Hymnal with 67 of the original Geneva Psalms. They are still being used, 400 years later, in the Protestant services in France.

H. Stein-Schneider

THE FIRST REFORMATION

The first French Reformation, which was clearly an attempt to separate the Church of Christ from its feudal trappings and to acquire for it a new freedom with a personal access to God, took place in the French city of Lyon, more than 300 years before Luther and Calvin.

In the year 1174 a certain Waldo (first name unknown), a rich merchant of that city, discovered that Christ had asked his disciples directly to "sell all their belongings, give the proceeds to the poor and follow Him" (Mtth.19:23). Taking this evangelical imperative to the letter, Waldo sold all his worldly goods, had the Gospel according to Matthew translated from the Latin into French, and began to preach the need for a more evangelical Christianity.

As he gathered disciples rapidly, his implied criticism of the feudal riches of the Church brought him soon into conflict with the Bishop of Lyon. Waldo and his group moved then to the South of France, from where the message spread quickly. In 1208 the Crusade against the Albigensians—whose spiritualistic beliefs the Waldensians strongly repudiated—gave the Catholics a pretext to massacre the Waldensians as "heretics."

After the holocaust, a small group remained in Southern France while the majority migrated to the high and inaccessible valleys of the nearby Alps, more secure than the open lands of the Rhone Valley. Stories on how the Waldensians descended from early inhabitants and perpetuated an earlier primitive faith, are folktales and have long since been discredited.

FRANCIS OF ASSISI was deeply influenced by the teachings of Waldo and his earlier call for total poverty. He received them almost certainly through his mother who was French (hence his surname "Francesco," which means "Frenchie") from the Rhone Valley near Lyon, and attempted a very similar Reformation in Central Italy in 1206. Yet his evangelical movement failed when it was taken over by the Roman Curia and made into a mendicant order of the Church.

In 1532, the Waldensians joined the Calvinist Reformation and suffered even more cruel persecution than ever before. Through a miracle, the Waldensians still exist today, after eight centuries of persecution, as an independent ecclesiastical group of the Reformed faith in Italy and France. Their headquarters are in Torre Pellice, near Turin, Italy. Huguenot groups from the United States have visited them. A Waldensian church and Seminary exist in Rome, on the Piazza Cavour, not far from the Vatican.

Some Waldensians migrated to the United States in the 18th century, mostly to Delaware. Names such as Bert, Bermond, Bonin, Flot, Griot, Lantelme, Pastre, Guyot, Jayme, and Pra belong to this earliest Huguenot movement of France.

JOHN CALVIN (1509-1564)

Born on July 10, 1509 in Noyon, northwest of Paris, John Calvin studied in Paris, where he was introduced to the evangelical ideas of Martin Luther by one of his cousins, Pierre Robert (Olivetan), who had studied in the free city of Strasbourg under Martin Bucer.

In 1533, Calvin obtains his Doctorate of Laws in Orleans and joins the evangelical movement. The first persecution of 1534 forces him to flee to Basel. There he finishes, at the ripe age of 27, his work about the basic tenets of the Reformation, the "Institution Chrétienne," in 1536. He then moves to Ferrara, Italy, where the court is won to the Reformation. On his way back to Basel in late 1536, he spends an evening in Geneva, where the local Reformer, Guillaume Farel, menaces him with the wrath of God if he, John Calvin, does not remain in Geneva in order to help him establish the Reformation there. Calvin accepts.

Yet Calvin's first stay in Geneva is brief. Intent on not only reforming the liturgies, but also the morality of the citizens, Calvin is thrown out by the local Burghers under a flimsy pretext in 1538.

Thus we find John Calvin soon afterward in the company of Bucer in the city of Strasbourg, where he preaches, in the church on Bouclier Street, to over thousand Huguenot refugees. Among those "Lutherans" is a young widow, Idelette de Bure, who becomes his faithful wife in a childless marriage.

In the meantime, the situation has changed in Geneva. Frightened by disorders in the city and by the enemies outside, the Council recalls Calvin, begging him to come back. This time they offer him considerably more freedom of action than during his first unhappy stay.

Thus, Calvin returns to Geneva in 1541, with definite plans to change this town in the image of the "Divine City" envisaged by St. Augustine, one thousand years earlier. In 23 years of arduous work, he molds the town and its inhabitants into a religious and political entity, completely motivated by Biblical faith and Christian ethics. Through a far-flung correspondence, through Geneva trained ministers, and through his many writings, Calvin deeply influences not only France, but also England and numerous other countries on the Continent. His message is not merely religious: By proclaiming the equality of all men before God, and the necessity of elected councils of government, he begins the revolt against the feudal royalty of his time and lays the foundation for the Democratic governments of the future, including the American Constitution.

Calvin dies on May 27, 1564 and is buried—according to his own wish—in an unmarked grave to avoid undue popular veneration of his earthly remains. The impressive "Wall of the Reformers," erected in 1936 in a Geneva park, not far from Calvin's Cathedral, is a monument to Calvin's worldwide influence, notably John Knox, the Scottish Reformer, who stayed with Calvin in Geneva and later founded the Presbyterian Church.

THE HUGUENOT TRADITION

The Huguenots were the followers of John Calvin. Their "tradition" is pure, unadulterated Calvinism as it was practiced in France in the 16th and 17th centuries.

Huguenot worship is characterized by its simplicity, its acknowledgment of sin, and its Bible-centered piety.

Pictures, under any form, are banned from the churches. Biblical inscriptions (Lord's Prayer, Ten Commandments) are on the walls.

Congregational singing is mostly Psalms put into verse by Clement Marot and Théodore de Bèze; music by Loys Bourgeois and Claude Goudimel.

The sermon is exclusively an explanation of a passage of Scripture, rather than a commentary on an article of the New York Times.

The vestments of the clergy are the Geneva gowns with tabs, (symbolizing the tablets of the law) which are the Bachelor's gowns in France at that time. Stoles and surplices are banned as "Romish."

The Lord's Supper is given with leavened bread and fermented wine. One large cup is used during the communion service.

Huguenot beliefs are based on the assertion of the total depravity of man and the impossibility of obtaining salvation by himself. Only Christ's sacrifice on the cross makes possible our reconciliation with God.

Predestination to both good and evil is based on St. Paul; it was also asserted by Thomas Aquinas. A good resume of it is in the Episcopal Prayer Book, p. 606, Article XVII.

Christ is present in the Lord's Supper through the "real presence," a position halfway between Lutheran realism and Zwinglian spiritualism. The faith of the partaker does make the presence real.

Huguenot church government is achieved through an elected church council. Though Bishops were never introduced into the French Church, the Hungarian Calvinists have this office in their churches.

Authority in the church is held by the judicatories: Council (local), regional, and national Synods decide. Between the sessions, authority is delegated to an executive council and its president.

Every member of the congregation is considered to be a minister and can therefore validly preach as well as administer the Sacraments. The Minister is only an "elder" with special learning and a calling, which has to be confirmed by the Church.

Huguenot politics are traditionally on the side of Democracy. With all men equal and equally depraved, leadership is synonymous with faith and moral rectitude.

American democratic institutions are Calvinistic. The Puritans of England were Calvinists who fled their homeland after the return of the Stuarts. These "nonconformists" laid the foundation for American Democracy of 1776. Thus, American democracy is basically Huguenot, via Cromwell and the Puritans, much too often maligned and misunderstood.

THE NAME "HUGUENOT"

The word "Huguenot" is of uncertain origin. Some historians insist that it is derived from the German word "Eidgenossen," which signifies "Confederates" in the Swiss political tradition. Its transliteration into French, according to an early 16th century Geneva document, is "eyguenots." Others believe that the word comes from "Hugues" a mythical rebel leader of the early Middle Ages.

There is, in any case, documentary evidence that the word "Huguenot" antedates the French Reformation. It was applied to the members of the Reformed

Churches after the unsuccessful Amboise coup in 1560.

The official name for the French Calvinists was R.P.R. (Religion Pretended Reformed) during the 16th, 17th, and 18th centuries.

Another name for the French Calvinists is "Parpaillots" (today mostly in jest) after one of the early martyrs by the name of Parpaille.

Officially, there are no longer any Huguenots in France. This name is reserved to the French Protestants prior to 1787.

THE HUGUENOT CROSS

The Huguenot Cross, formed by a Maltese (Languedoc) cross and connecting fleur-de-lis, above a descending dove pendant (signifying the Holy Spirit) became popular in Southern France, shortly after the Revocation of the Edict of Nantes, in the last decade of the 17th century.

A letter of the early 18th century, written by a Catholic priest, ascribes the "invention" of this piece of jewelry to goldsmith Maystre in Nimes around 1688 in Languedoc. The writer of this document surmises that the cross, which is not unlike the heraldic cross of Languedoc, was chosen by the Huguenots as a sign of their opposition to the "Latin" cross. The dove, he affirms, alludes to the prophetic movement (later to bring about the "Shakers") of the Cevennes mountains.

This speculation is sheer nonsense. Maystre did not "invent" the Cross. The design is taken very clearly from the

"Order of the Holy Spirit," a feudal decoration worn frequently by Henry of Navarre, the Protector of the Protestants, author of the Edict of Nantes, now revoked. Many pictures of Henry IV show him wearing it. The only "new" part is the place of the dove: In the Order of the Holy Spirit, it is superimposed upon the Maltese Cross, while the dove, in Maystre's Huguenot Cross, is pending. The change is minimal.

Today, the Huguenot Cross is not merely the insignium of the American descendants of the Huguenots. It is worn by all French Protestants, regardless of their origin. It is their "secret" sign of recognition. It is also worn by the Spanish and by the Austrian Protestants (both once persecuted minorities) who have adopted it as their religious emblem.

Among the French descendants of Huguenots, it is customary to give a small Huguenot Cross to every member of the family at the time of birth. One does not have to be a member of a Huguenot Society in order to wear it. It indicates a faith rather than a membership.

THE MEREAU

The Méreau was another traditional Huguenot symbol.

Every Huguenot had to present this quarter-sized molded pewter coin at the Communion Table in church on Sunday. Given out by the Elders the night before, during their visitation, it signified that the member of the Church was qualified to take the Sacrament.

Some of the original molds of the 17th century have survived and a small number of Méreau were made from them in recent years. They are however very rare, since they can no longer be produced without harming the molds. They show on one side the Good Shepherd in 16th century garb and on the other side an open Bible with the inscription: "Fear not, little flock."

THE FLAGS OF THE HUGUENOTS

There never was a Huguenot flag.

The Huguenots lived, fought, and died under the French royal flags. Their descendants used the French Tricolor.

The oldest royal flag used by the Huguenots was the royal blue pennant, with three large fleur-de-lis, of the Valois lineage of the Capetian dynasty. It was this blue flag, which was planted, together with Coligny's Admiralty pennant, into American soil in 1555 (Rio de Janeiro, formerly Fort Coligny) and in 1562 (Fort Caroline in Florida). This flag was therefore the second one, after the Spanish, in the northern hemisphere.

The white flag with many Fleur-de-lis became the Huguenot flag under Henry of Navarre, who was of the Bourbon branch of the Capetians. Henry rode into battle, with his Huguenots, on a white charger and wore a white panache on his helmet as a rallying sign. When Henry ascended to the throne, it became the royal flag. It was also the royal flag of his descendant, Louis XIV.

On July 15, 1789, during the early stages of the French Revolution—it was the day after the storming of the Bastille—Marquis de Lafayette, then vice-president of the Assembly, introduced at their meeting the Tricolor as the new flag of France. They are the correctly-read American colors, then a sign of order and democracy. The actual sequence of the American colors of red, white and blue, reads the American flag upside down, from the field up rather than from the canton down.

Since this "cocarde" was presented by Lafayette, the actual Liberator of the Protestants of 1787 and represented, during the Revolution the actual freedom of the Huguenots, the French Protestants consider the Tricolor flag of blue, white, and red, and not the royal flags, as their national emblem.

HUGUENOT HISTORY

1. *The Feudal Period (1536-1572)*

During the early years of the 16th century, the newly-found Biblical faith spread rapidly through France. In the beginning, the French Reformation attempted to adapt itself to the prevailing social order of Feudalism. John Calvin dedicated his "Institutes" to Francis I of France. Noblemen, won to the new faith, attempted to win over the court and perhaps also the King himself. Over-confidence spoiled things for the Huguenots early in the game.

When Francis found, in 1534, a printed copy (placard) of a diatribe against Holy Mass in his own apartments, he became scared and instituted the first persecution against the "R.P.R." He arrested in rapid succession about

150 followers of the new faith, carefully chosen among the lower classes. 27 were burned at the stake, 18 had their tongues cut out, and many recanted. In January of 1535, Francis published an edict, requiring the "extermination of the heretics" and promised 25% of their estate to the person who would denounce these "Lutherans" to the authorities. The great poet Clement Marot was forced to flee for his life to Ferrara, after having been denounced for eating butter during Lent. John Calvin fled the kingdom at the time of the "Placards."

On February 1, 1545, Francis had several thousand unarmed and Peaceful Waldensians massacred in Mérindol near Marseille. Their merciless murder aroused a great outcry of indignation in all of Europe.

In spite of these persecutions, the number of Reformed Christians grew steadily, mostly among the lower nobility, but also among the rising and overtaxed bourgeois of the cities, who saw in the Evangelical faith an opportunity to exert a much desired freedom and personal responsibility.

In 1546, fourteen "Lutherans" were burned at the stake at Meaux near Paris. The group is known as the "Martyrs of Meaux."

At the death of Francis in 1547, his son Henry II came to the throne. His wife was Catherine de' Medici, of the famous Florentine family. Though she was a niece of the Pope, she was not a religious fanatic, but merely a realist. She mainly wanted to preserve the throne for her children.

In 1559, the Reformed Church held its first National Synod at La Rochelle. It adopted a document of 40 articles, patterned after Calvin's theological views. It is known as "Confession de La Rochelle" and contains the basic beliefs, practices, and organizational charts of the Huguenot Church. It is to this day the basic confession of faith of the Reformed Churches of France - and thus of the Huguenots.

In 1560, at the death of Henry II—he died in a jousting match, with a lance through his eye—his son, Francis II became king of France at the age of 16. With such a young and inexperienced king, the feudal factions rose their ugly head, attempting to gain power and perhaps even the crown. The Huguenots were the "Progressives" and the Catholics the "Conservatives" in the ensuing struggle.

Thus, the fight was on between the Guise family, champion of the Catholic faith, and the Conde clan, who had espoused the Reformed cause. The attempt of the Conde faction to bodily kidnap the young king away from the henchmen of the Guise, ended in disaster, with the mutilated bodies of the Huguenot noblemen dangling from the balconies of Amboise Castle in 1560. The young king died the same year, leaving the kingdom in deep turmoil.

Ten-year-old Charles, his brother, could not become king. So his mother, Catherine de' Medici, took over as the Regent of France. With a woman at the helm and the king too young to have his say, the Feudal Lords had a free-for-all, mainly under the guise of religion.

In order to appease the factions and save the crown, Catherine at first attempted compromise. She appointed as her chancellor Michel de l'Hôpital, a moderate, who advocated reconciliation between the Catholics and the Protestants. In order to explore the possibilities of such an understanding Catherine invited Théodore de Bèze, Calvin's right hand man, to a public debate at Poissy on September 9, 1561. Neither side scored decisively.

Soon however the Guise faction, opposed to compromise and reconciliation, took the necessary steps to prevent a rapprochement. On March 1, 1562, the troops of the Duke massacred a whole Huguenot congregation at Vassy in Lorraine. The Huguenot noblemen met the challenge and rose in armed resistance. In the course of a series of conflicts,

Guise was killed by a double agent and Conde died assassinated at Jarnac.

Finally, the moderate views of Admiral Gaspard de Coligny prevailed. He attempted reconciliation from a position of strength. As a true statesman he realized that the Huguenot cause, of which he was now the leader, could not prevail on the battlefield. His ultimate aim was to win the king over to the side of the Huguenots through peaceful influence.

Coligny also imagined a positive solution to the religious problem: Peace would be assured by placing a whole ocean between the warring factions. The Huguenots were to found, on the newly discovered continent of America, a French Kingdom of Protestant faith. He thus sent 600 Huguenot colonists to Florida in 1562, where they founded Fort

Caroline, the first and oldest settlement in North America. They ran afoul, however, of the territorial ambitions of the Spaniards, who massacred 500 "Lutherans" at Matanzas Inlet.

In France, however, Coligny's plan worked only too well. As Coligny's influence upon the young king grew, Catherine and the Guise panicked. As a first attempt to assassinate the Admiral failed on August 22, 1572, and the king ordered an investigation of the circumstances, which would have uncovered Catherine as the real author, the Regent organized, cold-bloodedly, the St. Bartholomew's Night Massacre. On August 24, as almost all the Huguenot noblemen were assembled for the wedding of Henry of Navarre, she told her son that they had come to take over the palace. She had Coligny assassinated by her Swiss guard and instigated the massacre of all the Protestants who could be found both in Paris and in the provinces. 10,000 Huguenots perished.

In Rome, Pope Gregory XIII had a special Mass of Thanksgiving said in celebration of the murder of the Huguenots and a special medal was struck to commemorate this "great victory."

2. The Democratic Period (1572-1628)

Suddenly deprived of its leadership, the Huguenot movement could have shriveled up like an old apple. It could have curled up and died. It did not. It merely came into its own. The Huguenots merely reorganized with a new leadership, namely the up-and-coming middle-class of France. These new leaders were the merchants and the artisans of the cities, crushed by taxes, which they and the farmers were the only ones to pay in the kingdom. They organized their church no longer according to feudal lines of the court, but according to the new democratic ideas emanating from Geneva. Theirs was the first organized attempt at Democracy in the history of France.

Forced against the wall, Calvinism showed its true political colors, which were decidedly Democratic. They even succeeded so well in their organization along those lines that they frightened the autocratic rulers of France and became the victims of the backlash. The king, so far mostly afraid of the feudal lords, now had to worry about one more potential enemy: The Huguenot State within the State which Henry IV had created with the Edict of Nantes. The new Republic fell victim to Richelieu in 1628.

Charles IX died in 1574. He was succeeded by Henri III who in turn was assassinated by the Guise in 1589. Since there was no male heir, the crown fell to his nephew, Henri of Navarre, the leader of the Huguenots.

A Huguenot king? At first things seem to work out. But Henry's Huguenots cannot take Paris, which is defended by a Spanish garrison. Yet, in order to be king, he must be its master. Thus, on July 25, 1593, Henri de Navarre declares, "Paris is worth attending mass once" or something to that effect, and "converts" to Catholicism. He is crowned king of France under the name of Henri IV at St. Denis, near Paris.

At first, Henri IV does little for his former friends and associates. Then, in 1598, he promulgates on April 13, the Edict of Nantes, which guarantees the religious and political freedom of the Huguenots.

In the religious realm the Reformed Church can hold services in certain French cities and on the lands of over 3,500 noblemen of the Reformed faith. They must pay their taxes to the Roman Catholic Church, but the Catholic Bishop has to pay the pastor's salaries and other expenses of the church.

In the political realm the Huguenots receive a certain number of fortified cities, where Reformed garrisons can be kept. There they have their own schools, their hospitals, their democratically elected Councils. They are a state within the state, a Democracy within the Kingdom.

This dream of a Protestant Republic ends with the death of Henri IV. In 1610 he is assassinated by a fanatical monk who believes that the king has sold out to the Protestants.

Louis XIII (1610-1643) appraises, quite correctly, the provisions of the Edict of Nantes as a grave restriction of his royal power. He sees with suspicion the growing influence of the free Huguenot cities, such as Montpellier and La Rochelle.

In 1624 Louis XIII choses as his chancellor and *alter ego* (both have goatees) Cardinal Richelieu. Their common determination is to do away, as soon as possible, with the political power of the Huguenots. Royal garrisons are established in strategic locations near the Protestant cities and the civic freedoms are whittled away one by one. Finally, in early 1628, Richelieu puts simultaneously the siege to Montpellier and to La Rochelle. Both fall to the aggressor, after a heroic defense, late the same year.

Thus the political power of the Huguenots, crucial to their survival, is broken. What is left is pitifully little. The Huguenots are from this point on without defense against the encroachments of the local Bishops, who can always secure a royal decree in their favor. There is no hardcore persecution—yet. But many Huguenots *see* the handwriting on the wall. After the destruction of their "Republic," their days in France are numbered.

3. Religious Period (1628-1685)

Louis XIV succeeds his father at the tender age of five, in 1643. Anne of Austria, his mother, becomes the Regent. She chooses an Italian, Jules Mazarin, also a Cardinal, to be her wily Chancellor.

At the death of Mazarin, in 1661, Louis XIV begins his reign, the longest in French history. He dies in 1715, after having reshaped France and her government.

Distrustful of the Paris merchants, whose revolt (la Fronde) had him and his mother flee the Louvre in 1648, he displaces the royal residence to Versailles. Intent on taming the Feudal Establishment, he proceeds to its virtual elimination. But rather than dismantling the Feudal Lords by executions, he makes the most independent princes an assembly of lackeys, who vie for the honor to carry the king's chamber pot. He concentrates decision-making in the huge complex of Versailles and could well have said:

"L'État, c'est moi" (The State, it is I).

His desire to dominate completely the conscience of his subjects and to eliminate any possible resistance against his autocratic regime brings him from the very beginning into conflict with the Huguenots and whatever is left of the religious and social provisions of the Edict of Nantes.

Though the Edict of Nantes was made "irrevocable" by Henri IV, his grandson simply suspends one provision of the Edict after another. Churches are destroyed. The holding of Synods is forbidden. Protestants no longer can hold a large variety of offices, or exert influence on many regulated professions. These are only a few of the numerous vexatory edicts concerning the members of the "P.P.R." Yet their spirit remains unbroken, their faith and their churches are strong.

The next step is religious terror. Failure to kneel when a priest passes with the Sacrament in the street brings the demolition of the Reformed Church at St. Hippolyte du Fort in Southern France (Feb 24, 1681). Huguenot cities where freedom was established by the Edict of Nantes are taken by the army, the churches are razed, and the services prohibited (March 6, 1679). Huguenot children are systematically taken from their parents in order to be educated in convents as Catholics (January 31, 1682). Yet, the Huguenots are forbidden to leave the country (royal edict of May 18, 1682).

Finally, there is the forced conversion. A special fund, the "Caisse Pelisson" is created, in order to induce conversions through material advantages. If this does not produce the desired results, there is a much more convincing way to convert the Huguenots: The Dragonnades. This consists in stationing soldiers (dragoons = royal Cavalry) in ever-greater numbers in the Huguenot home. They destroy the house, rape the women, and ruin the family financially. Mass conversions are recorded wherever the quartermaster appears.

At the beginning of 1685, hardly any provision of the Edict of Nantes remains in force. As long lists of "conversions" are presented at Versailles, the king has them counted. There are more conversions than there ever were Protestants in the kingdom. Louis XIV concludes: since there are no longer any Huguenots in France, there is no need to keep on the books any law concerning them. Thus, Louis revokes, with the stroke of his pen, the irrevocable decree on October 18, 1685.

THE WALLOONS

Strictly speaking, the Walloons are not Huguenots. There is a slight but important difference between them.

The Walloons were French-speaking Calvinists who came from the part of the Hapsburg Empire, which is the southern part of Belgium today. Directly persecuted since 1589, they migrated largely to Holland, where they founded a number of French-speaking churches.

When the Huguenots arrived, almost a century later, they found a warm welcome among the earlier French-speaking refugees. Many of these churches (they call themselves "Walloon Churches") are still thriving in Holland even today. French is still the language spoken at the services. Among their members, however, there is no difference between Walloons and Huguenots. The distinction is merely historical.

Some of the Walloons came over to America at an early date, together with the Dutch. Thus, the first governor of the city of New Amsterdam who bought Manhattan from the Indians for a few trinkets was Pierre Minuit. The legend of the twenty-four dollar price is a play on the name Minuit, which is the twenty-fourth hour of the day. The French "Huguenot" church was very definitely a Walloon church when it was founded in New Amsterdam in 1627. Families such as the Rapalje (no descent from nobility) as well as the De Lannoy are of Walloon rather than Huguenot origin.

In 1924, the United States issued a series of three stamps commemorating the "tercentennial of the arrival of the Walloons and in honor of the Huguenots."

1. The Huguenot "Underground" (1685-1787)

The Revocation of the Edict of Nantes drove the Huguenots "underground." Many fled the country; but even a greater number stayed. Those who remained endured unspeakable hardships.

Deprived of their civil rights, non-persons before the law, illegitimate in birth, deprived of a daylight funeral in death, they could not hold any public office or pass on an inheritance. Possession of a Bible or hymnbook was punished by years in prison. Those arrested at secret church services were condemned to the galleys, to row until their death. Ministers were simply executed.

Yet any of them could have integrated into society easily. All that was required was to attend Mass and sign a piece of paper. Many refused.

Others made the gesture in order to spare the ordeal from their children. This was the case of the Huguenot named Barthélémy Giscard, who presented himself to the Priest at Marvejols in 1710 to be married. His children were baptized into the Roman church, but Barthélémy remained away from Mass until his death in 1760, when he was buried as a Huguenot. This Barthélémy Giscard is the direct ancestor of the President of the French Republic, Valery Giscard d'Estaing.

During these 102 years "under the cross," assemblies of Huguenots were held in private homes and in openings in the forest, in the "Desert." Itinerant ministers encouraged the "little flock." They studied in Geneva and Lausanne, which were also called "Schools of the Martyrs." None of them died of old age. In Montpellier alone more than 35 ministers were put to death in the town square.

An armed revolt, fanned by a prophetic movement, known as the "War of the Camisards," raged in the Cevennes Mountains in the South of France during the first decade of the 17th century. Sustained by their enthusiastic faith, the Huguenots resisted successfully and obtained finally to be left alone and "ignored" by the authorities.

Two deeply moving shrines of the Huguenots "under the cross" can still be visited in Southern France:

Aigues-Mortes, with its Tower of Constance, was the prison for women, whose walls were ten feet thick. Marie Durand, incarcerated there for 35 years, engraved on the parapet of the well in the middle of the room the word "RESIST."

The Mas Soubeyran, also called "Museum of the Desert," is located in the Cevennes Mountains a few miles west of Anduze. It contains excellent exhibits and poignant documents of the period, complete with a hiding-place for the minister in case of a police search. On the first Sunday in September 10,000 descendants of Huguenots meet there for open air service, a Lord's Supper with the chalices of the 17th century, and a huge joyous picnic. Church-chartered buses come from all the regions of France and from other European countries. The ceremony is transmitted by both radio and television all over France.

After Louis XIV's death in 1715, the political and religious climate in France change considerably. Philosophers such as the volatile Jean-Jacques Rousseau, the impetuous and devastatingly witty Voltaire, and the meticulous Jean le Rond d'Alembert, led France to a climate of reason and toleration. Slowly even Versailles felt the need for a greater freedom of thought.

Voltaire helped the Huguenots decisively. In order to show the utter folly of tyranny and bigotry, he took up the posthumous defense of a Huguenot from Toulouse, Jean Calas, who was tortured to death for a crime he could not have committed. In a press campaign as famous as the one of Émile Zola for Alfred Dreyfus, 100 years later, Voltaire obtained Calas's rehabilitation; his son, banished for life, was able to return from Geneva. Suddenly France became aware of the fact that there were still some Huguenots in their midst, and that tyranny and superstition were the cause of their unjust suffering. After the "Calas Affair" there were no longer any death sentences meted out to Huguenots. But they still remain without rights and are non-persons before the law and the birth registers which were kept by the Catholic church. The insecure Louis XVI refuses to change anything the "Sun King" had ordered.

Help comes—of all places—from the United States. The Marquis de Lafayette, returning from the War of Independence, finds the situation of the Huguenots intolerable. American Huguenots were his friends. He had been welcomed on American soil by Commander Huger, a Charleston Huguenot and his friends. He had fought side by side with them during the war. Many of them were fellow-Masons. Upon his return to France, he wrote George Washington:

"The Huguenots are subject to an abominable despotism. Their marriages are illegal; their testaments have no legal value; their children are considered illegitimate; they have no legal rights. I would like to bring about a change in the

situation. This is an undertaking that will take time and which presents some major inconveniences for me. Nobody is willing to give me a letter or help in any way. I am determined to go ahead nevertheless."

Thus, Lafayette obtains from Louis XVI, singlehandedly the "Edict of Toleration" of November 7, 1787, which guarantees the Huguenots a new freedom. The state "tolerates" Huguenot worship and the legal existence of Huguenots—simply by not mentioning their illegality.

Only two years later, in 1789, the French Revolution brings total and unconditional freedom to the Huguenots. Suddenly and unexpectedly several hundred thousand of them surface in

France. A century of dire persecution has not been able to eradicate their faith!

Napoleon brings both Catholicism and Protestantism under the protection of the government. From now on until 1905, the Protestants receive large subsidies from the government. A prestige church, the "Oratoire du Louvre" is given to the Protestants; it is in front of this church that a large statue of Admiral de Coligny is placed, by popular subscription, during the 19th century.

Today the descendants of the Huguenots constitute a very active and well-recognized minority in France, about 2% of its population, but with an influence much larger than its actual size. Denominations have united into the French Church Federation in 1939, in which the French Reformed Church is the largest member church. Freedom and equality are assured for all believers.

THE HUGUENOT DISPERSION

Strasbourg, in Alsace, a free city, was the earliest place of refuge for the persecuted Huguenots. Calvin moved there in 1538 and became the Pastor of the French Church there.

Geneva, another Free City also outside of the French frontiers—but not part of Switzerland until 1848—became the rallying point for the Huguenots under the leadership of John Calvin ever since 1541. In fact, they arrive in such numbers that they practically take over the government during the lifetime of Calvin and remain in command for almost four centuries.

The German Princes open up their lands to the Huguenots after the devastations of the 30 Years' War in 1648. Most of the Reformed Churches in

Germany are of Huguenot origin. Certain first names, handed down faithfully in many families, are a heritage of the Huguenots—such as Marie-Louise and Annemarie. Prussia and Frederic the Great attracted the Huguenots and gave them commissions in the army. Thus, even Adolf Hitler's Wehrmacht had in its ranks a large number of Generals with French names of noble origin.

Holland, where the Walloons had established their churches, became a haven of refuge for many, including the de Coligny family, from whom the actual reigning family is a direct descendant.

Ireland really hit the jackpot. The Huguenots introduced the linen industry to the Emerald Isle.

England subsidized the Huguenots very generously with liberal gifts from the Crown. London's Huguenot Church of Soho Square was chartered in 1550. Other Huguenots worshipped in the Crypt of Canterbury Cathedral, where Cardinal Odet de Coligny, Bishop of Beauvais, murdered in 1571, is buried. Cardinal of the Roman Church at the ripe age of 16, he was the first member of the powerful de Coligny family to convert to the Calvinist faith.

The American Colonies also became an early place of refuge. Nicolas Martiau arrived in Elizabeth City in 1620. He settled in Yorktown in 1631, became the owner of what was later to become the battlefield of 1781, and became, as well, the French Huguenot ancestor of George Washington on the Warner-Reade side.

As land and work for Huguenots in Europe became scarcer after 1670, opportunities in the British Colonies beckoned. Yet coming to the Colonies was not as simple as one might imagine it today. Money, and a lot of it, was required of those who wanted to come to America as free citizens rather than indentured servants. One had to pay for the voyage on the pier; money was needed for building materials, seeds, and farm animals of all sorts. Artisans needed rent money and raw material for their trade. One had also to provide funds for food during the first year in the Colony, or at least until the first successful harvest. Quite often therefore, the English Crown subscribed to these expenses. The group of Huguenots who arrived on the Richmond at Charles Town in 1680 were supposed to cultivate silk worms and plant vineyards, since those items were then imported at high cost from France. Their voyage was paid by the Crown and every effort was made to set them up on parcels of land not far from the port city.

Language was also another barrier for the new immigrant. Unless the Huguenot could make himself understood in English, there was little opportunity for him in trade. He had to make do with a parcel of land to cultivate and hope for the best for the next generation, whose lot would improve with the years.

Thus, we find relatively few Huguenots attempting to settle as isolated immigrants. Multi-family groups who were able to raise the money or to find a rich sponsor for them were quite more frequent.

Most of the Huguenots came therefore as a group, a French village, complete with a French Church and a

Pastor. Such was the case of the Huguenots of New Paltz who had formerly found shelter in the German Palatinate. They settled in the State of New York. A magnificent restauration of the original houses gives us an insight into what a French community of that time was like.

Chastain family

<u>In Virginia, a similar group received land that had belonged to an extinct Indian tribe, the Monacans. Thus, the Huguenots called their settlement "Manakin Town." The descendants of these Huguenot immigrants are grouped in a Huguenot Society of their own.</u>

In South Carolina the Huguenots arrived at the newly-founded city of Charles Town, but were promptly shipped out to the boondocks in order to provide food and stock in trade for the port city. Contrary to expectation, however, rice became their most desirable export.

Within two generations, also, the Huguenots were back in the city, where they had established their Huguenot "Meeting-House" (only the Church of England was allowed to call its place of worship "church"). The Huguenots, having become prosperous, moved back into the city and eventually took over the town commercially and socially. They also founded the oldest still active Association in the United States, the South Carolina Society. It was established by the Huguenots in 1719 in order to help the ailing business of a tavern owner by the name of Poinsett, and later on, other Huguenots as well. Toward the end of the 18th century, the Society became the bastion of the French language, where the well-educated families sent their children in order to have them learn the language of their Huguenot ancestors. Today the South Carolina Society is a social gathering, but indeed the oldest of all Huguenot Societies, by far.

Once English became the vernacular of the Huguenots, they changed their church affiliation from their French speaking churches to American congregations. Most of the Huguenots identified with the official church of the Colonies, the Episcopal Church. Only a small number united with the Presbyterians (Scottish Calvinists). Economic and social considerations presided in this choice rather than theological affinities.

Only the Huguenot Church in Charleston, South Carolina, remains as an independent congregation. Founded in 1684, it kept both its independence and its Neuchatel liturgy. Even during its leanest years, the French services were continued once a year by the actual author of this "Brief History." Every year the church was filled to the last seat on the last Sunday in March, reserved for the Huguenot service with liturgy in French and sermon in English. This was the tradition for more than 25 years. In 1980 the Church Council took the giant step to establish weekly Huguenot services and to employ a regular Minister on a fulltime basis. The reports that have reached us before this edition went to press seem to indicate that the church is building up, with attendance that is regular and almost better than expected.

Thus continues, on the shores of this New World, the tradition of the Huguenots. It is a story of faith and suffering; of steadfastness and persecution; then of God's blessing and success. As we look back, we cannot but admire these men and women of faith and their Christian beliefs for which they were ready to lay down their lives. Theirs was a faith of which we can be proud, because it is our own.

Made in United States
Orlando, FL
07 July 2023